THOSE
Left
Behind

My Brother's Suicide

C.A. Blake

BALBOA.PRESS
A DIVISION OF HAY HOUSE

Balboa Press books may be ordered through booksellers or by contacting:

Balboa Press
A Division of Hay House
1663 Liberty Drive
Bloomington, IN 47403
www.balboapress.com
844-682-1282

Because of the dynamic nature of the Internet, any web addresses or
links contained in this book may have changed since publication and
may no longer be valid. The views expressed in this work are solely those
of the author and do not necessarily reflect the views of the publisher,
and the publisher hereby disclaims any responsibility for them.

The author of this book does not dispense medical advice or prescribe
the use of any technique as a form of treatment for physical, emotional,
or medical problems without the advice of a physician, either directly
or indirectly. The intent of the author is only to offer information
of a general nature to help you in your quest for emotional and
spiritual well-being. In the event you use any of the information in
this book for yourself, which is your constitutional right, the author
and the publisher assume no responsibility for your actions.

Any people depicted in stock imagery provided by Getty Images are
models, and such images are being used for illustrative purposes only.
Certain stock imagery © Getty Images.

Print information available on the last page.

ISBN: 979-8-7652-4696-2 (sc)
ISBN: 979-8-7652-4698-6 (hc)
ISBN: 979-8-7652-4697-9 (e)

Library of Congress Control Number: 2023920867

Balboa Press rev. date: 10/31/2023

Dedication

To my sisters Suzanne and Brenda
and my daughter

Contents

Contents

Those Left Behind: My Brother's Suicide

I awoke with the phone ringing at six in the morning. Even as a twenty-four-year-old, I knew it wouldn't be good news. And it wasn't. It was my mother. She told me my brother, Steve, was dead. He had shot himself outside his girlfriend's apartment the previous night.

I suddenly heard a horrible scream and realized it was coming out of me. I could not comprehend the message I had just received. I scrambled out of bed, got dressed, and dressed and fed my child. She needed to go to preschool, and I needed to keep it together until she left.

I did, but when she left with her dad, I jumped in my car and drove hysterically to my brother's friend's house with the expectation of some answers. I received none. His friend was unaware of the event. Then I drove to the site of the incident, Steve's girlfriend's house.

Of course, I expected to see a crime scene, and imagined I would be the hero who brought the wounded back to life. But there was no body, no blood on the pavement, no police outline, and no yellow tape, just me standing there in a daze, outside in the cold. I was the wounded.

It was a cloudy and cold October morning. It was quiet—no one around. This all seemed surreal to me. I couldn't believe it was true, couldn't make sense of it. If Steve's life had been so great, he never would have thought to do something like this: leave me.

Childhood Memories

My brother, Steve, was almost two years older than me and always quite a handful, in a good way. Full of life, generous, and kind, he possessed some magnetic force field around him that drew so many to him. He was a talented artist and musician, and very good looking. Men and women alike were attracted to him. As a child, he had visible skills of charm and persuasion. I will always wonder if he'd had a different early life, would he have wanted to live longer?

Our parents were not your typical role models. Oh, they did the best they could, but it seemed difficult for them to consider their two young children with any consistency. Steve got the brunt of our father's alcoholic aggression, and I received the lion's share of my mother's neglect. We were pretty much on our own, and it was actually better that way.

Steve was completely responsible for me in the early years—responsible and in charge. He would watch out for me and coerce me into going along with his mischievous adventures around the neighborhood. We would climb trees, cut through neighbors' yards, and jump off garage roofs. Not really my first choice of how to spend the day, but I followed him without question.

Sometimes we would go to the cliffs, sneak behind a metal fence, and walk around on a path that dropped straight down to the railroad tracks onto a rocky beach. One of our neighborhood friends slipped and almost fell off the edge. Steve and I pulled her up while she was grasping at tufts of grass and bushes. It was a close call—one incident that we never told anyone about, either. When things didn't go well for Steve, he could find a way to salvage the situation. In this case, he saved our friend.

Steve could usually get me to do things

I was not really brave enough to do and quite a few things I didn't really want to do either. There was a fearless component to his adventures, the memory of which has stayed with me all these years. I'm still impressed I made it through some of them without a scratch. Steve was less fortunate, but he never seemed to mind. He would shake himself off and start some new adventure.

The dependency between my brother and me necessarily grew very strong. He was the one who came to my bed when I was sick and held my hand when we crossed the street. He brought me to school for subprimary orientation and showed me around, as he was already a well-known character in first grade. As the older brother, he was protective of me most of the time. Later, I became protective of him too.

We grew up in New England and attended school two years apart. Steve seemed to have a lot of trouble his first couple years. He got into difficult situations. From my little-girl perspective, everyone seemed to be picking on him at school. This is about the time our roles switched. I became more protective of him, filling in the gap our parents left open. Steve was always a handful, and I was always impressed.

One typical incident occurred when he accidently knocked over the huge fish tank in the main hallway of our elementary school. He was running around the hallways and banged into it, and the whole thing smashed to the ground and shattered, fish fluttering around on the floor at the main entrance to the school. This fish tank was the school's signature display, representing the best aspect of the school for inner-city kids. The loss was a huge scandal, of course, and Steve was punished. This was just one of his many misadventures that I recall.

When he was in second grade, I saw Steve being hurled through the air by a sixth grader. I ran home to get Mom, but she wouldn't come to help him. We were on our own. I ran back to Steve, crying hysterically, helping him off the pavement, and I got him home.

He was bleeding in various places, but he was still punished for getting in the fight or for losing it or something along those lines. I was beginning to see a trend. Children see and learn. I was learning to be responsible and alert. Steve was too.

The following spring, Steve was able to salvage his reputation by winning an art competition for the school's new facade. His drawing of children playing hopscotch was etched into the front of the school, larger than life. Even when he was a child, his artistic talents were visible. That's the way he was, a villain and a hero. I believe that artistic project was a factor in keeping him in school that year. After all, he was a genius.

During that time our family was quite poor. The children next door were not allowed to play with us. I thought it was because we were out too late at night. But I think now it was because we were always messy and getting into trouble. It didn't bother me; I just noticed. In those days, we didn't have any complaints and few concerns. We were kids and we had each other.

Mom was not the best of cooks in those days. Canned spaghetti and fried bologna were specialties. One "supper" event included liver and onions. I wouldn't finish the liver, due to the gagging response it caused. My brother ate his and left the table. What a showoff! Moments later he was whisper-yelling to me in the window from the yard next door that happened to be visible from my seat at the table. There he was, bolder than life, taunting me: "Psst, throw it out to me! I'll get rid of it."

Well, that seemed to make sense. I had been sitting alone at the table for what I thought seemed like an hour, staring, and trying not to smell that gross liver. *Look at that thing! It's hard as a rock! I couldn't chew it if I tried! I'm just a kid*, I thought.

After I determined an appropriate amount of time had passed and Mom had her back to me in the kitchen, I chucked that gross piece of liver out the window into the yard next door. Imagine mother's surprise that a large, cold, dried piece of, well, an organ, had disappeared completely from my plate within minutes. Wow, it was a miracle.

But look out the window. There was Steve, my big brother, the mastermind with the evidence, which he picked up off the ground before making his getaway. I never knew what he did with that thing, but as always, he was resourceful. He'd make it up as he went along. He was a genius and my protector. As a child, I often worshipped him and desperately needed him.

Summer in New England provided endless opportunities for fun. We could climb things, collect worms, and, when Dad came home, we'd collect the neighborhood kids and have a raucous baseball game in our gravel yard. Steve, of course, was the star player. I was too small to run the bases alone, so Dad would pick me up and drag me around them. No matter—I was playing with Steve and the neighborhood kids. I was part of the gang, and my big brother was the leader.

We had a lot of outside commitments as kids. Steve was on the basketball team, and I was a cheerleader. We had to walk a long way to get to the games. We'd usually go together, and our team played pretty well. Sometimes it was treacherous getting home in the dark in all kinds of weather. But it was a relief to make it home. Our parents never came to the games, but we didn't mind. We had each other.

Our home was an apartment with two bedrooms. Steve and I and our gerbil shared one room at the back of the apartment, and my parents shared a room in the front of the apartment. Luckily, we didn't have much contact with our parents. They seemed busy with other things most of the time. When our younger sisters arrived, we helped take care of them, often with mixed results. A few mistakes were made, but we all got through them. Steve was committed to teasing our sisters a lot. It was pretty funny.

When our house was condemned, our family moved to a large single-family home a couple of towns away. I had just finished fourth grade and wasn't too keen on the move. I still remember the new house well because it has continuously been the source of many nightmares to this day.

This new house seemed to have a hundred rooms, and a huge yard with actual grass and trees on it. It had a driveway covered with tar and was a block or so from the beach. Steve and I quickly discovered we could go through the neighbor's yard to the next street, go over the hill, and make it to the area known as the "cliffs" overlooking part of an abandoned shipyard. This became a sacred meeting place, and we played there a lot in all kinds of weather. Of course, we never told our parents about it. We had learned not to tell about stuff that would get us in trouble. Fortunately, they never asked about what we did during the day.

Steve and I climbed around the cliffs and had awesome adventures. Naturally, he was the leader. But as I became more expert at negotiating the terrain, which included high walls and rocks spilling into the ocean, I would bring some of my school friends around. Well, I actually only had one at the time, and after she slipped off the wall onto a pile of old auto parts below, she terminated our friendship. I had saved her life, but I guess it just wasn't enough.

Our Home

It was fortunate we had outside places to play, because the house itself was creepy and always under some major construction. My father built and rebuilt stuff all the time, and he was always in a bad mood while doing it. It was particularly brutal to watch my brother try to help him. My dad seemed to think Steve could never do anything right and the effort usually ended in an argument of some sort. I learned to avoid the scene altogether.

Fortunately, that first summer, Steve and I were shipped off to a farm to pick some kind of berries for cash, about fifty cents a box, if I recall. We would walk about ten or fifteen minutes down the road and wait for a red pickup truck to pick us up. Into the back we would go, and ride, for what seemed like hours, to huge fruit and vegetable gardens. Did I mention there were also spiders in that field?

My terror of spiders at the time was greater than that of falling off the cliffs at the fort, so I can only imagine the origin of that fear. In my adulthood, my mother confessed that I had learned spider fear from my father. That could be true, although there was little discussion about any family characteristics and traditions in my house, and I was surprised at the leak in the facade.

As an example, we had always been told we were of Scottish descent until I was well into my teens, and someone slipped and said that my dad had an Irish family background with some Native American blood mixed in. Decades later, I found out I wasn't even related to him. My mom had had an affair with an Italian musician, and I was the product of that union. I don't think my fake dad ever knew. He treated me as if I was his own daughter. I'm sure it was better that way. Such is family life.

So, back to the farm. I was terrified every day, picking fruits and vegetables and being on the lookout for the feared daddy longlegs that inhabited the plants. My big brother and I were separated most of the time, so I was on my own. I was probably nine or ten by then, but I was still terrified of all manner of bugs. Anyway, wasn't it illegal for children to be farm workers on someone else's farm? Whose idea was that?

Thankfully, Steve the Man, as he was becoming known, did a courageous and very intelligent thing—he started cheating. He would put rocks, grass, and who knows, possibly some daddy longlegs in the bottom of the baskets and covered them over with berries, then turn them in for money. He was making a fortune. I only learned later that it was the reason he had been asked to leave that industry for good. So, I had to go alone without my protector. I didn't quite understand what had happened until later, but I knew cheating was unacceptable. How did he think to do that?

Meanwhile, terror of terrors! It was just me and a million spiders waiting for me, pretending they had an interest in farming. It was a conspiracy. Thankfully, the folly of sending a ten-year-old female child alone to a farm miles away from home in the back of a pickup truck was considered, and someone (it could have been the government) asked me to stay at home. Whew! Steve was in big trouble, of course, mainly because we lost a chunk of the family income.

Fortunately, school began after our robust summer activities, and we moved into our different cliques. I lost touch with my big brother when he got into high school and started hanging out with the cool kids. He was a talented guitarist in a popular rock band. He was a stud, so to speak, and every bit the babe. I think that was about the time he started some risky behaviors, as all teenagers do; being cool is a lot of work.

Steve used to sneak out of his second-floor bedroom using a ladder my father had set up beside the house for repairs. Often, when he returned from a night out, my dad would be waiting for him, and they would argue and fight. Sometimes my mom and I would get involved. It was always a messy business.

It's safe to say Steve and my dad did not see eye to eye on anything, and it was unpleasant to be around them. I sometimes got caught in the fray by accident, so I learned to avoid the home scene. I vanished into adolescence and my world of school, after school activities, and a part-time job at a local jewelry store, where my life opened up. School and work provided a wonderful diversion from all the chaos at home.

It was rare that Steve and I would hang out together when we were both in high school, and our family continued as usual, except my mother was diagnosed with multiple sclerosis during that time. I had two younger sisters to watch by then, and now my responsibilities included keeping an eye on my mom and caring for the home. Steve had a job, and he had enrolled in college classes. Unfortunately,

dad asked him to drop out of school to help
support the family financially.

Time passed. I graduated from high school,
turned eighteen, left the family home. After
a year of living with girlfriends, I traveled
to Europe for three months with my future
husband, came home, and got married. I had
my daughter later that year and instantly
became a traditional homemaker. I was
twenty-one and had no clue what I was doing
most of the time. Nevertheless, I loved it.

I lost sight of Steve in those days except
for times when either one of us needed
something. We would occasionally visit each
other, and he even lived with me at times.
He would often stop by and play baseball
with my daughter in the yard, and he always
had his guitar with him, ready to play a new
song he had just learned. Whenever I needed
help, he'd show up and check on me. I tried
to reciprocate and keep my eye out for him,
too, but we seldom talked about anything
serious, and I always knew he could handle

anything. We just showed each other a quiet, consistent love.

As years went by, he began having more troubles, but I didn't recognize the depth of them. Steve always had a way of making everything look so easy and casual. But I guess things weren't so good after all. He was struggling with his girlfriend and had recently lost a job. I knew he would get through his current trials, as he always did—until he didn't.

He called me from a local emergency room one spring day, and I went to meet him, his girlfriend, and a psychiatrist treating him in the emergency room. I knew the doctor. I worked at the hospital at the time. The doctor said Steve was having difficulties, whatever that meant, so I tried to keep a closer eye on him as best I could. It seemed a bit of an intrusion given the dynamic of being his little sister, and we were both adults now. But we kept in touch more often. I also took it upon myself to hide Steve's hunting rifle, which was in my apartment at the time. I hid it in the trunk of my car and forgot about it. In fact, I forgot about the whole incident given the changes he made in his life.

Months past and Steve's life improved immeasurably. He stayed with his girlfriend, got a job, and seemed happy and carefree. I visited him when I could, and he came by our apartment more often and hung out with our friends. When Steve and I were alone, we would talk about God and express gratitude for the good things in our lives. I knew he had turned a corner, and I began to relax about his welfare. There was no reason not to. It seemed Steve was enjoying life.

It was during that time that some of his friends made plans to go deer hunting and invited Steve to go along. So, guess what I did? I told Steve where his hunting rifle was. He brought it into my house and left it in the spare bedroom to clean it. He had taken it apart and it lay on the floor in the corner of the spare room in pieces for weeks.

In the middle of the night in October, Steve sneaked into my house, grabbed the rifle, and took it with him to his girlfriend's house. He was waiting for her to come home. She was apparently out with another guy. Of course, I could never confirm that report. There was no one to ask. The police report stated that Steve faced a car coming up the driveway to her apartment and had a rifle in his hand.

Apparently, his girlfriend and another person were in the front seat. They got out and went into the apartment together, leaving Steve outside alone in the driveway. The police report stated a robbery had been called in by the resident of the apartment at about the same time.

When the police arrived at the scene, they recognized my brother. The cops and my brother had gone to school together. Steve was sitting on the front steps of his girlfriend's apartment building with the rifle pointed at his chest. I was told the police report said Steve was talking to the policemen when there was the squeal of an approaching squad car, and Steve jerked back, causing the gun to go off. I always thought his death was my fault. I had given him back that gun.

Following that early morning phone call from my mother about Steve's death, I went to the emergency room to find his doctor as soon as I had a presence of mind to do so. I marched into the hospital and screamed at him and asked why he couldn't have helped my brother more. He was, of course, horrified. He had apparently been working with Steve for a while and was quite fond of him. I'm sure this death by suicide had a big impact on the doctor's life, too. It was such a tragedy.

As a result of the horrible event of my brother's death, the hospital created the first outpatient mental health clinic in the town. This was in the 1970s. Too late for Steve, who had apparently been trying to get help for some time, but I'm sure it has helped many others after him and continues to operate to this day.

After the Death

About two hundred people attended my brother's funeral. It was an unusual event to have a suicide in our town, which is what everyone believed had happened. My mom did not attend the viewings, due to the worsening of her multiple sclerosis symptoms. She had a relapse and could barely make it to the funeral because of the stress of the loss of her only son. My dad struggled to comprehend the reality of the situation and was shrouded in disbelief and denial.

I have very little recollection of the funeral myself. I remember seeing some of his friends run up to the casket, shouting in disbelief. There was a lot of crying; few words were exchanged. I couldn't control myself much of the time, either, but I had to pull it together as I was designated as the greeter for the arriving guests and had to take care of the other details specific to such events.

I had made the arrangements for my family at the funeral parlor and purchased the clothes Steve wore in the casket at the mall. I bought him shoes but wasn't sure he needed them. His feet didn't show. That was sad. I bought him a cross necklace to wear in the casket. I cut my hair short, for some reason, and drove around aimlessly during the days of the viewings. I attended the wakes and the funeral as the primary family representative, making sure everything was taken care of. I was twenty-four years old. I had lost my best friend and my hero. I had no idea what I was doing, and I blamed myself for his death.

I had seen death at my job in the hospital, but not of someone I knew. I had never had a close loss. I was unprepared for the lasting impact my brother's death had on me. Steve was the most important person in my life, might still be. Our relationship was the closest I had come to an understanding of the meaning of being cared for and loved. I was not prepared to understand why this had happened. I did not have enough information and could not forgive myself for letting this happen. I carried enormous guilt, assuming I should have done more to prevent his death.

I had helped him, protected him, and loved him all my life. And I always trusted he would be OK. We were both strong and brought up to take care of ourselves. It's taken me a long time to forgive myself for letting him know about the hunting rifle. I am surprised I can even write about it. But my guess is there are other people left behind who also regret the things they did or did not do for their lost loved ones. The regrets are like having a permanent tattoo; they don't go away. The answer to the question about his intention can never be resolved.

My family didn't discuss Steve's death. After the funeral service, only a handful of the two hundred friends and acquaintances from the wake and funeral attended the "reception" at our house. No one wanted to be too close to the situation. There was nothing to say and at the time there was a certain stigma associated with taking one's own life. The profound suddenness of the event was difficult to fathom, and no one really knew how to handle it.

At the funeral reception at our home, my father played badminton in the yard, seemingly oblivious to the horror of the event, and, of course, he drank. I hated him. He made my brother think he was a loser, and I held my father partly responsible for the tragedy. I ultimately thought it was Dad's fault that Steve didn't think much of himself.

My brother was buried on Friday, October 13. I don't really remember going to the cemetery. I don't remember much about it to this day. I did order the flowers for the grave and wrote his obituary. I think that's where most of my recollection about the funeral comes from, something I had written about it, not the actual event. I remained in a haze for a long time. I couldn't shake it; I was paralyzed by disbelief.

Most of my family was in denial about what had happened, too. My mom had found Dad at his girlfriend's house the morning of Steve's death. She asked for a divorce from her husband of twenty-seven years that day. After we cleaned up from the reception, we went to our respective rooms and homes. My father went to his girlfriend's house. Nothing more was said.

The family home was eventually sold, and we all scattered into our own lives. I did not speak to my father for years after Steve's death. Dad continued to try to drink himself to death. It was a harsh punishment, which I don't think he could ever resolve, but Dad never seemed to blame himself for anything related to Steve's death. I did visit Dad a few times before his passing. He welcomed me with open arms, as if nothing unusual had ever happened in our lives. We did not discuss Steve or anything related to the event. Although I harbored feelings of blame for him, I was later able to make amends for my decision to cut dad out of my life years later, at his graveside.

I always felt I should have been the one who saved my brother, or at least helped more than I did. I was working in surgery and taking psychology classes at the university, so I guess I thought I should have been some kind of expert on saving lives. But I never thought Steve could have possibly been serious about not liking himself. I loved him so totally. Everyone did.

A week after the funeral, I went back to my day job, saving lives in open heart and trauma surgery. My daughter went back to her school; my husband went back to work. I continued psychology classes at night. There were no words to express my sadness. I felt empty. I couldn't comprehend what had happened, and I couldn't understand why it was taking me so long to get "over it." The pain was enormous, and the whole thing was surreal.

During the years following Steve's death, I couldn't bear my own reality. I became a nonhuman. No feelings, no one to talk to about it. It seemed no one could relate to such an unholy event. I stuffed it like all the other members of my family and probably some of his friends, too. Suicide was an infrequent and taboo subject in those days. My Christian upbringing led me to believe my beloved brother was forever in hell. It was a scary concept. Not much of a transition for Steve, not much for me to hold on to. This shattered my faith in anything.

In my psychology classes, I was looking for answers. I screamed at God whenever I got the chance. The denial and pain grew so large, it wrapped itself around me, and along with other changes and losses in my life, I had nothing left of myself to hold on to. I had abandoned myself at my brother's graveside. There was me *before* his death, and now me as a shroud, *after* his death. My early life before Steve's death wasn't that great, for sure, but afterward, I became some kind of emotional phantom. The funny thing is I didn't notice it until years later, when my own life came to a halt.

Those Left Behind

With so much sudden and traumatic loss in our lives these days, I knew it was time to write about my own traumatic experience. I am not alone with such a loss anymore. I don't have to hide or be ashamed or embarrassed, and neither do you. These days, there are many of us who are left behind for a myriad of reasons. We're comrades in pain, struggling with grief and loss.

It's in the news daily: shootings, gang violence, stabbings, terrorism, unexplained plane crashes, drug overdoses, veterans and cops committing suicide, people getting shot in bars and movie theaters, children in schools, 9/11—all these incidents leave people behind to manage the ugly pain associated with sudden, unexpected loss.

After the funerals, the cards, and flowers, the guests leave, and the loved ones and friends are left alone to manage their grief over the long haul. It's not pretty, and it's not easy. The intense pain doesn't pass quickly, and the wound never heals completely.

Initially, I spent a lot of time blaming myself and others for not helping Steve enough. I had a spiritual practice before he died, and he and I prayed together shortly before he took his life. We were thanking God for his new job and that he was moving back in with his girlfriend. His life was turning a corner. But within a few months, he was dead. I could not understand that and still struggle with it.

There's no denying it's possible that a suicide victim had an unhappy life, right? My brother had all kinds of problems I wasn't even aware of while he was alive. Our childhood was challenging but we didn't care that much. In my young adult perspective, I didn't understand the depth of his struggles. He always shrugged them off. In the 1970s, Steve's substance abuse didn't stand out much either. It was a trend among the youth at the time.

After his death, I naturally hated God. Yes, I'll say it out loud. I hated Him and blamed Him. I couldn't save Steve, but God should have. So, my beloved brother, who watched out for me and was my hero, was now in eternal hell according to a wide spectrum of religious ideologies. You can see my dilemma. Taking a life is not a high point of most spiritual practices and is often looked upon as unforgiveable. Potentially, others left behind have to figure out a way to live with a similar dilemma.

We might have to create an argument in our minds for our loved ones' salvation, a justification for things we have little or no understanding about. Sometimes we have to rely on some of the dogma offered to us as children, which might no longer fit. The mental and spiritual struggle that comes with unexpected death causes much pain, and in my case, guilt and shame. I didn't realize it until years later that I felt ashamed of the whole thing. I was embarrassed for a lot of reasons.

In the case of suicide, it's not always considered that fault lies on the victim's shoulders. I had elevated my brother to near saint status, remembering all the details of the heroic deeds and kind acts he did for me and others. And he was so much fun to be around and so talented. I didn't notice his flaws or his struggles. He always seemed fine and would laugh things off easily. So, I blamed myself and others, not him.

These days we seem to have tragedies on a regular basis and many of us are the ones left behind, suffering quietly years after the events, pretending we're the same person as before the event. And yet, we are scarred; scarred with memory, loss, guilt, and sadness. I felt strange in my inability to get over such losses, as if there was something wrong with me. I just had to accept my deficit and move on.

The horror of 9/11 shook the whole world. Just hearing about it caused suffering for those who were not even involved personally. I was a responder. I knew more than a few of the victims personally and many who were left behind. At the time, I was struck again by the weight of unexpected tragedy. It added another layer to my almost perpetual grief. I knew it was another load for many others to endure, too. We all needed support.

Those left behind have something in common. How in the world do we go on living with such losses, such grief? I think the closer the loss, the worse those left behind suffer. Of course, we can't show it because it falls outside the socially acceptable standards of expression. Therapy helps for a while, if you can afford it, but afterward it is just you and your scar.

Those left behind share similar stigmas. We blame ourselves and often feel responsible in unrealistic ways. We are often an angry bunch, wanting someone or something to blame. We hope someone or something will help us, too. We want to run, to hide from a pain so deep it scares us to be alive.

Challenged by the events and mitigating factors contributing to the loss, and with no means of expression, we are also challenged by our beliefs or lack thereof, about ourselves and our God. Nothing makes sense anymore, and we can lose the strength to struggle with concepts and belief systems. We can become troubled and despondent. Time does heal, but not enough. One doesn't completely get over such things. Just ask the remaining veterans from previous wars. Decades later, they still cry at the memories of things they saw, things they remember, and the pain of loss. Indelible memories wound tightly around the heart.

A Simple Tale

A year or so before Steve died, I was on call at the hospital and went in to work for an emergency open heart surgery. The patient had had cardiac arrest at home hours before and was brought into the hospital by ambulance. Our surgical team performed beautifully, trying to save the patient's life. As hours went by, it became clear the patient wasn't going to survive. It was about three o'clock in the morning when I had the certain feeling that the patient was no longer in his body on the operating table. I felt like he was looking down at us in the operating room. There was no question about this in my then unreligious mind. It was just what was happening, and it was a rather peaceful feeling. I sensed an afterlife at the time.

The patient was pronounced dead shortly thereafter.

I have carried the memory of that feeling, that knowing, with me all these years, with no question or explanation for its occurrence. I didn't even notice how natural it felt. I've never been one for the supernatural, being such a fearful individual. I didn't want to know any more than I needed to, nor did the experience open any spiritual inclinations. The boundaries around my physical form were enough for me to handle. But I do remember the event of that night in detail. The feeling of the patient being present in another form above the room comforted me even during the tragic situation. It opened my awareness to what might be possible.

The Road Back to Myself

My journey to some semblance of mental equilibrium took years. In the first years after Steve's death, I took antidepressants but got bored with them. I was still working in surgery at the time of his death, so I was familiar with death, but not loss. Surely, not a personal loss like losing my brother.

The experience with my brother changed the way I handled death and sickness for all time. I had also relinquished all belief in a higher power and allowed a quiet fury to reside in the place God had once held. I see now how deeply I felt that loss, too. With no higher power, I was on my own, trying to figure things out, mostly about how to live with such pain and always wondering what I could have done to help Steve.

I cried a lot. I screamed in my car on the way to and from work when no one was around. Time was passing since Steve's suicide, and I didn't understand why I couldn't get over it. I went to therapy, blabbing away about my miserable history when I dared to actually describe it. I'm sure I had diagnoses of all kinds, and most therapists were terrified I could be suicidal, too. I never was, for some reason. I wasn't mentally ill. I was just grieving. Sometimes the powerful emotions of grief felt like insanity.

I resisted feeling the actual depth of the loss, I think. I touched it a few times shortly after Steve's death, but I was too afraid I couldn't handle it, and that I would become a blathering, depressed person, unable to function in the world. So, I toughed it out. I faked it every day and every night for many years, until I couldn't anymore. Until it caught up with me and brought me to my knees. And on my knees, I cried to the very God I had forsaken so many years before and hated. He was still there.

My prayers at the beginning were the usual anger and vitriol I often spewed out at "something" outside myself. Frequently accompanied with obscenities and beginning with the ubiquitous scream, *Why?* I realized how often I had always spoken to the God I hated after Steve's death, but not in a nice way. Nevertheless, I was crying out to something, blaming and criticizing the very power that created me.

The screams had become less about Steve and more about me. This was a dramatic and downward shift in the process of my unresolved grief. Why was I so messed up? I was a good person. Why didn't God prevent this? What was going to happen to me? Was I going to make it through this morass? Where was the loving God? It turns out the prayer-screaming was OK. God could take it.

My Healing

My transition into a peaceful spiritual being was a long, drawn-out process that continues moment to moment to this day. After my brother's death, I began searching for answers about, well, God. How dare He (I use the masculine pronoun) relegate all suicide victims to eternal hell? What about those unrepentant souls who couldn't make it to confession before they died? I've *never* been to confession. What does this mean for my future afterlife?

I began to question and study. For my brother's sake, not mine. Religion, philosophy, anthropology (in case other cultures had different views about death), new-age books, old Eastern spiritual texts, Upanishads, Bhagavad Gita, the Tao Te Ching, self-development books, and of course, the Bible, including newer versions such as the Book of Thomas and the Book of Mary Magdalene. I studied *A Course in Miracles* and many spiritual teachers who offered positive affirmations and healing thoughts, such as Louise Hay.

I had never dared to meditate before, as the religion of my youth taught me that "an empty mind is the devil's workshop." At the time, being a fearful woman-child, I didn't venture into the world of what I considered to be the mystical. I continued to use many versions of denial and avoidance, even during this spiritual seeking period. The accumulation of information wasn't soothing my guilt and grief.

I wasn't seeking to change myself or use the information for my improvement or redemption. I was seeking to prove God wrong and to put organized religions in their place. I had no interest in becoming religious or spiritual myself. I had accepted my specialness, my scar, and I buried any feelings regarding it. I was only on a mission of discovery. When I had moments of despair, and there were many, I ran into hiding emotionally and in any way I could.

I realize now what courage I had to do this alone. Of course, I contracted into myself, closed myself down. But I also looked for ways to keep my heart open to others and to help those I could, a balance for the chasm I felt between myself and everyone else. I was still very sad and very guilty. Nothing said otherwise.

Fortunately, I had the blessing of a beautiful daughter, and I could focus on being a good wife and mother. During those years, I also had other responsibilities to keep my mind diverted from the discomfort of loss, so I learned to stuff my feelings, deny their existence, and avoid them. It was natural for me. I had grown up that way, I was an expert. And what a good job I did.

After fourteen years of marriage, I divorced my husband, growing tired of his infidelities, and struck out on my own. I received an academic scholarship to a wonderful college and jumped at the opportunity to finish my education. I worked hard and graduated on the dean's list. The following year, I was invited to apply to a medical school for employment and education. Looking back, I think it was fortunate I did not receive the job. So, I moved to the city I had always wanted to live in, New York City. I had no plan, no permanent residence, and no job, but three hundred dollars in my pocket and a lot of enthusiasm.

I began a string of low-paying jobs in the medical and art fields, found an apartment, and I gutted it out for a few years before I began moving up the ladder to some kind of corporate life. I was keeping myself busy from myself, away from my past, and I loved it. Working was fun for me. It kept me occupied. Leisure time brought trouble and I was uncomfortable with it. I didn't know how to handle it.

Eventually, I became a health-care executive, and I loved the job. I worked to improve the standard of care for New Yorkers and was proud of my accomplishments. After September 11, 2001, my well-developed facade began to leak. I was a responder and experienced many losses of colleagues and friends. I searched for them and helped those who survived. The event was terrifying and immeasurably sad. I spent months looking at the rubble with hope waning as time went on. I salute those lost there and the families left behind. I understand how they felt, and still do. The survivors' losses continue today.

Six months after 9/11, my beloved mother died, and not in a good way. The hospital she was admitted to had neglected her and altered her medical record regarding her condition. It was near the hospital where I received my medical training and the one where my brother received his psychiatric care. At the end of my mother's illness, my sister called me and told me to come to the hospital as soon as possible. When I arrived hours later, my mother was unconscious. She died early the next morning. I was never able to say goodbye to her. I had arrived just in time to see her die. I later opened an investigation related to her death.

Three months after that, my father died in the home he shared with his girlfriend, the woman he was with when my brother passed. The mourning continued. I had seen Dad months earlier and was able to say what I needed to say to him. There were many things I was proud of him for, including his World War II service in the navy. Both of my parents had grown into wonderful people at the end.

Meanwhile, my facade was crumbling and crumbling fast. But I was able to hold things together until I lost my job. It was the one thing that provided an identity for me for nearly twelve years. Afterward, there were no new job offers, even with my best attempts. Time marched on and I was alone in my small apartment during the day with a lot of the time on my hands, no plans, and, of course, I was afraid. I didn't know what to do and had no one to ask.

It wasn't until my adult daughter's near

suicide attempt over a relationship breakup a couple of years later that I hit my knees. I finally had to stop and ask, *What is going on'? Why wasn't God doing what I wanted Him to do? Why this again? Why, why, why?* This was way more than I could handle. She was my only child, and she was suffering. I was terrified for her and went to comfort and support her. Over time, she got through her difficulties and continued her successful life in Boston. Her healing had begun and continues to this day. But I had become overwhelmed with anger and now operated from a platform of chronic fear.

After a while, I realized, screaming about things to something I didn't believe in wasn't helping, so I enlisted the help of a professional life coach and future friend. She encouraged me to hope and offered me some coping skills, which I began to practice daily. Even though I was angry a lot and didn't understand what had happened to me, I knew I was a good person. I always tried so hard. But now I really didn't have anything to hang on to, so I listened. I read books. I kept a journal, and it wasn't pretty. I learned to meditate; I cried a lot, spent a lot of time alone, visited my favorite oak tree in the park, walked, and took deep breaths.

My coach suggested I make plans for something that would bring me joy. I couldn't remember what that word meant. I was in so much pain. She suggested I keep something I thought was beautiful near me. So, I bought a crystal star and kept it with me, studying the way the light touched it. It helped me smile. It reminded me of beauty. That's all I could do at the time. Sit and look at the crystal and try not to freak out. It had been so long since I had thought about things that would help me feel peaceful. But I was OK. I was right here, right here. Breathe. Begin again. That's all could do.

I was surprised to learn that my coach had known my brother from high school. They had a mutual friend. That was some coincidence. She had known about his passing in real time. It was somehow validating for me after so many years of denying I even had a brother.

No one in my New York life ever knew, and I wasn't about to bring it up.

After working on myself with my coach for some time, I made the dramatic and courageous decision to treat myself. I flew to Rome for rest and exploration. I had wanted to return to Italy for twenty years, and now I was doing it, taking care of myself and honoring a long-held desire. "Treating yourself like a precious object helps you heal," I was told by my coach, and I was going for it. It was do or die time for me now. I couldn't take any more drama. I surrendered. I was letting go. I needed a change of scenery. And I was terrified.

In Rome, I think I went to every church in the city and cried and prayed for the better part of ten days. I don't even remember what I was praying for—just a release from my suffering, I think. It was beautiful there, and I tried to learn how to take it easy. I explored the city and often needed lunch at the wrong time for Italians, around three o'clock, when most places were closed.

One afternoon, I found a café that was open close to my hotel and ordered a pizza. I was the only one in the place. The waitstaff were setting up tables with umbrellas outside, and I was inside watching their efforts through the window, facing the street.

As I was devouring my amazing pizza slice, I looked up to notice a group of people waiting to cross the street in front of the restaurant. A nun in an azure blue habit was in the group of about ten people. As they passed, the nun turned and looked directly at me through the window. She continued to look directly at me as she walked by. She had a kind and loving aura about her.

She was young and beautiful, and I watched as she passed, struck by her attention. Moments later, as I continued my lunch, I became aware of a tingling sensation rising through my whole body. I couldn't understand it, but it was delightful and comforting. Suddenly it occurred to me she had blessed me, and this was the feeling of love. Perhaps my prayers were being heard after all. This must be the feeling of joy. It was another life lesson for me to recall many years later, and I still refer to it often, the memory of that joyful sensation when I was alone in another country.

Later that week, I found an English-language bookstore by chance. One of the featured books was the *Power of Now* by Eckhart Tolle. I had tried to read this book before and couldn't comprehend the message, and now, there it was, waiting for me in another country, no less. I took it to lunch with me and underlined meaningful passages. Was this another coincidence? I'm not sure I understood much of the book at the time, but it was pleasant and provided some direction and rest for my weary soul. The trip had been a long-held dream, and I was pleased with myself for having the courage to go alone. I was also writing in my journal and learning to sketch. I was softening to the concept of a higher guidance.

Upon my return, I found myself focusing on my daughter. I feared for her when she decided to go on a road trip alone. I soon found myself falling into an abyss of what felt like madness. It turned out to be a deepening fear that easily connected with my past. What if she died? How could I help her? She was hours away, and I didn't exactly know where she was a lot of the time. Was she unhappy? Was it my fault? Did I fail her, too?

This thinking was creating another whole set of problems. I was losing myself. Crying became a daily routine, and I was lost, really lost this time. A friend recommended I go to a twelve-step program. I think she was tired of listening to my anger and complaining. The program I went to was for people who grew up in alcoholic and dysfunctional homes. I qualified and I went. I went almost every day. What else did I have to do? I had no job, little money, and I was alone in Manhattan during the day stressing out about everything.

In the program, I think I cried every day for a year. I cried mostly about Steve, my dearest brother, the first and biggest loss in my life. I had never really dealt with it, pushing, pushing it down all those years. I cried for myself, too. I had been in such denial about my sadness and about my own childhood. Making believe it was normal or acceptable because I was tough, a mother, a wife, a student, and working, working, and moving ahead. I didn't know I wasn't taking care of myself. It didn't occur to me. I just didn't know how. I learned how in those meetings.

These things are learned slowly and over time. It's not uncommon to hit the ground before seeing that changes need to be made, that there's even a choice. But there are choices, and the beauty of it is that the choice is easier than the struggle not to choose. I was told the universe is not doing stuff *to* you, but *for* you. I was being saved by something greater than myself, and I had to help by letting go of my grief and struggle. Taking care of myself first, before others.

I guess that seemed selfish at the beginning, what with so many less fortunate than myself, including my daughter. She was in her thirties now and struggling, too. It took me awhile to realize we had the same options. We were both adult women struggling and looking for answers. We were each in charge of our own life. I was not in charge of hers anymore, and she wasn't in charge of mine. I learned I'm in charge of my own life, and no one else is. I was responsible for it. It's a sad day when you finally get that—a sad and a wonderful day. It's usually precipitated by some kind of fall; usually a loss, sometimes many losses.

Fearful as I am, I didn't want to look within, but when the grief, anger, and false pride subsided to manageable levels, I noticed there was a sweet, gentle person inside. It was me. The real me was beautiful. No job, crazy family, no hobbies, plans, or income, and yet I was as beautiful and sparkling as I had ever been. Like my crystal. The only difference was now I was aware of it, and a smile crept onto my face that has not left since. I just had to stop for a while, and look inside myself, to just be.

My Thoughts

A sudden loss can shake up a person, and we handle it as best we can. Dealing with it includes a whole range of behaviors and thoughts. I hid for as long as I could. Avoidance and running away were hallmarks of my early life as a child in a dysfunctional family. I still run sometimes. But now I do so with gentleness, and then I come back to myself. Pema Chodren, the wonderful Buddhist author, would say, "Coming closer to yourself." I can now look at myself with less judgment and more compassion. I've made peace with myself and family, and now I understand they were doing the best they could. Me too.

As I was growing up, I had learned to have unrealistic expectations of myself; so did my brother. I am still here, he's not. And now I almost dare to think that his death helped me to recognize the magnificent person I am today and always was. I see now, that as a caretaker, I might have lost myself in helping him out of the troubles he constantly created for himself. I did try to rescue him for most of our lives together. It was difficult at times. It would have been hard to keep up that pace and I recognize the toll that could have taken on me and my family now that I look back. His loss also taught me about love, a deep abiding love.

There's a beautiful teaching I recently read about. Souls agree to help each other when they get a human life, like a contractual agreement before coming into human form. The reading suggested that sometimes sacrifices are made for the other souls in the group for the greater good. The idea pleases me. I could be the product of a beautiful sacrifice by those souls who loved me and still do. Maybe they couldn't make it to this point, but they knew I could. They might be angels now, watching over me. So, I'm going to be the best version of myself in this life, just in case it's true. It's a better option than not believing in myself and their wisdom.

I no longer believe in hell. I no longer believe in a punishing God. I no longer hate my God, either. He and I have an easy coexistence now. As Wayne Dyer explained, "God is the ocean, and we are a cup of ocean water." How beautiful. I'm hanging on to that image. It's beautiful to imagine being part of something so magnificent and mysterious.

It means I am in the heart of God, and so is my brother, and my daughter, and so are you, already. There's nothing we need to do; we are already in God's embrace. We were made that way in the beginning of our life. We just forgot our beauty. And it takes a long time to get it back, to remember. Sometimes people we love have to push us in strange ways to this realization. I'm not sure I would have come to it without all the loss and pain.

My expectations for myself were always unrealistic, but I didn't know it. I feel I have achieved all that I set out to achieve and more. And I have done it honorably. It's just the perfection thing. I couldn't forgive myself for perceived mistakes. Although I could never name them, I had a vague sense that there were tons of them. Well, there aren't; that's why I couldn't name them. I have a few really deep scars that I created myself, mostly as an adolescent, of course. But living with the haunting feeling that something was wrong with me and that it was my fault just wasn't accurate; it's part of the legacy of growing up in a dysfunctional home.

My star crystal symbolizes the beginning of my long climb into presence. Here I am, choosing to move forward without regrets. I had many teachers along the way, some kinder than others. I think my daughter has been my greatest teacher, and I don't yet know the fullness of the teaching. Something about love, detachment, and compassion, I think. At least that's what I'm learning today. I'm also learning about patience and self-forgiveness. I'm learning about self-love.

I now see my greatest responsibility is for my own life. Not Steve's, not my adult daughter's, not the gentleman on the operating room table. My job is to love myself first, and if I do, I will have much more love to share with others. I just don't have much control over whether other people live or die. It was never my choice to make.

I believe the great sadness of those left behind can evolve into great compassion. We can love others who suffer because we ourselves have suffered, and we understand it. That's what Jesus showed us, the Buddha, too—and probably many other teachers. It's all about love. It always was, and it begins with loving yourself.

I still experience sadness now, but not only sadness. I feel compassion, as well, compassion for myself and others. I feel a love that acknowledges we are all part of one whole. I think that's why Jesus wept. He watched and felt the same sadness sometimes, feelings of sadness for others with compassion. We have many opportunities to practice this range of emotions now, to turn the corner of our pain into something kinder.

Some humans can't find their peace on this earth. I'm hoping they get another chance later on, maybe somewhere else. I'm comforted by the possibility. I'm grateful I've had some unexpected experiences that reminded me to keep moving toward peace and joy, and to wonder at the mystery and magnificence of life.

A friend of mine who is a security guard at my art school said to me the other day, "Can you feel him? He's right next to you."

I was in a busy hallway and looked around me. "No," I said.

"It's someone who loves you very much," she replied. "He's right next to you. I can see him. My family can do that. He said he loves you and he's watching over you. Light a candle and say a prayer for him." Tears streamed down my face, and I knew she was referring to my brother. It seemed to be message from above, an otherworldly message that freaked me out and comforted me at the same time.

It was hardly a message I expected from

her, as we didn't know each other very well. But I considered the possibility that my brother's spirit was there and might be closer than I think. What would be the harm? And how did the security guard know I had such losses? We had never spoken about such things. I just listened and wondered. The incident expanded my perspective about life, like the nun in Rome and the man on the operating table who passed. I was opening to the possibility of grander thoughts about the universe. There's a complexity to life beyond my understanding. I don't always need to understand.

I did exactly what my friend said. I prayed for Steve at a nearby church and lit candles for him and for my daughter, too. I still do. I hope someone does it for me when I pass. I do this for love, not only the loss. It's an offering of gratitude for the way I love them and for the message of hope and possibility it holds. It felt good to hear that my brother might be watching over me still.

Other Thoughts

I think it's a good time to consider ourselves, our loved ones, and all sentient beings as what Jesus said we are—part of God, whatever we perceive God to be. And our perception of being part of God might just be better than the perception we have of ourselves without it. So, you could say it's a higher power of some sort, higher than ourselves.

Those left behind need to keep searching for something to help them switch off the pain and blame once in a while, a pause. Perhaps you can imagine the possibility of a gentle guide who looks after you from above to give you a rest. It's OK to rest after a loss and stop some of the noise. It's OK to be just who you are, scars and all.

These days, I am honored to grieve for my brother, my parents, my 9/11 friends, other loved ones, and friends who have passed. I feel sadness *and* I celebrate their lives. They were like us with their struggles and good intentions. What if we are all the heroes, gurus, and saints? What if we get to return someday to be a guardian angel or a spirit guide for those we loved? I like to think I have a lot of angels watching over me these days.

My brother was no less my hero because of the way he died or the things I have since learned about his life. My love for him was not diminished by the violent act of his death. I have loved him unconditionally. It's taken me years of being one left behind to be able to figure that out, and now I add myself to the list of people I love unconditionally. It's a sacred love for us all.

I also forgive myself for being a twenty-four-year-old woman who couldn't understand the ramifications of his struggles. I forgive my family for not helping enough, and I love them anyway. They, too, were doing the best they could, and I'm proud they did as well as they did. I now know that their early lives were not picnics, either. I am saddened by my understanding of what they all went through.

It's called compassion, and it hurts because I love them. Now my tears represent personal growth and a quiet acceptance of what happened to us. I cannot change past events. I cannot change other people, either. I have learned to hold the pain of loss and the gift of love at the same time. I will continue to try to live with an open heart.

Lately, I can shift into joy for having known and loved my beloved, messed-up brother, and I love him still. That's what remains with me now—the memory of the feeling of love. And I can share that feeling of love with myself for having gone through so much. I made it, and it was hard, and I am better able to understand why others don't. I also know it's worth the effort, to ease into healing for yourself and others who love you.

We all suffer and some of us are gifted with the ability to endure. Some of us are gifted with the ability to fall to our knees in utter despair and be lifted, somehow, by a power greater than ourselves, even one we don't believe in or love. As the Tao Te Ching says, "All of life is a movement toward our Wholeness." I'm considering that possibility. I continue to grow into my wholeness despite the losses.

Those left behind deserve the honor of our own love. Maybe a piece of the love we gave to the ones we lost remains for ourselves. Maybe our loved ones want to give it back to us once they moved beyond our world. Maybe we can learn to give love to ourselves with time. Maybe our love can grow unconditionally. Maybe the losses have shown us how to be tender with ourselves and others. It's something we need to practice daily—being gentle with our suffering selves so we can continue to heal.

The Beginning

I went back home for a family wedding a few years back. I still felt the anxiety associated with my loved ones and our history. This time, I didn't feel the need to visit cemeteries where my family members were laid to rest. It was a short visit, and I didn't feel up to it, probably never did. This time I asked myself what would be best for me now. I never asked that before. I could visit the graves on my next visit when I might be stronger.

I believe those we lost would want us to love ourselves more, consider our own needs more, and they would want us to love others more, too. It's OK to cry for them. I hope people cry for me when I'm gone. These tender qualities keep us human, and left behinds have more special qualities than most. God needs us here, to touch others for Him. That's why I'm writing about this. I hope it helps another who has suffered loss of any kind. We deserve our own compassion.

The challenges of my childhood taught me resilience, I guess. We all have it. We all have learned many fierce lessons over the years. We probably have more to come. Our perspective can change over a lifetime and soften, I think. It has for me. I now have more gratitude for what I have experienced and achieved. I have more compassion for myself and others who have suffered, all others. And all others *have* suffered. As Wayne Dyer said, "Your ability to know the power of kindness and love most likely grew out of some darkness and pain in your past."

Love yourself in this moment, flaws and all. Be the sad, lonely person you feel you are and move forward gently. Love yourself just the way you are now, one moment at a time. Your transformation will take time and just might contain the richness you and your loved one believed in in the first place. It's worth the effort to possibly be inspired by the fact *you* are the one left behind. Sparkle for yourself and those you love. They somehow added to our ability to do so.

We are a divine expression of life and so are those we have lost. They might just be smiling at us from a place of peace and joy. They might be praying for us and hoping we turn around and face ourselves with a smile and a hug. If anyone knows we need it, they do. Don't give up on yourself. Don't give up on them, either. Love is everywhere.

> Every blade of grass has an angel
> beside it whispering grow, grow.
>
> —The Talmud

The Prophet

Then a woman said, Speak to us of Joy and Sorrow,

And he answered;

Your joy is your sorrow unmasked.

And the selfsame well from which your laughter rises was oftentimes filled with your tears.

And how else can it be?

The deeper that sorrow carves into your being, the more joy you can contain.

Is not the cup that holds your wine the very cup that was burned in the potter's oven?

... when you are joyous, look deep into your heart and you shall find it is only that which has given you sorrow that is giving you joy.

When you are sorrowful look again in your heart, and you shall see that in truth you are weeping for that which has been you delight.

Some of you say, "Joy is greater than sorrow'" and others say, "Nay, sorrow is the greater.

But I say unto you they are inseparable." (Kahlil Gibran)

Bibliography

Buddha: *Dharmapada*

Wayne Dyer: *Manifest Your Destiny*

Foundation for Inner Peace: *A Course in Miracles*

Kahlil Gibran: *The Prophet*

Louise L. Hay: *You Can Heal Your Life*

The Bible

Laozi: Tao Te Ching

Eckhart Tolle: *The Power of Now*

Pema Chodren: *Comfortable with Uncertainty*